# Groovy MANDALAS

COLORING BOOK

SHALA KERRIGAN

DOVER PUBLICATIONS, INC.
MINEOLA, NEW YORK

Mandalas are symmetrical designs that represent the universe, and are used as a tool in meditation by many cultures. These carefully constructed patterns bring enlightenment to the viewer. Originally found in the ancient teachings of the Buddhist and Hindu religions, the timeless mandala is recognized throughout the world for its spiritual content as well as its enchanting beauty. Inspired by the psychedelic 1960s, the thirty-one mandalas included here all feature such groovy symbols as peace signs, beadwork, flowers, and even the smiley face. The pages in this book are unbacked so that you may use any media for coloring, and are perforated for easy removal.

*Copyright*

Copyright © 2014 by Dover Publications, Inc.
All rights reserved.

*Bibliographical Note*

*Groovy Mandalas Coloring Book* is a new work, first published by Dover Publications, Inc., in 2014.

*International Standard Book Number*

*ISBN-13: 978-0-486-78343-7*
*ISBN-10: 0-486-78343-X*

Manufactured in the United States by RR Donnelley
78343X09 2015
www.doverpublications.com

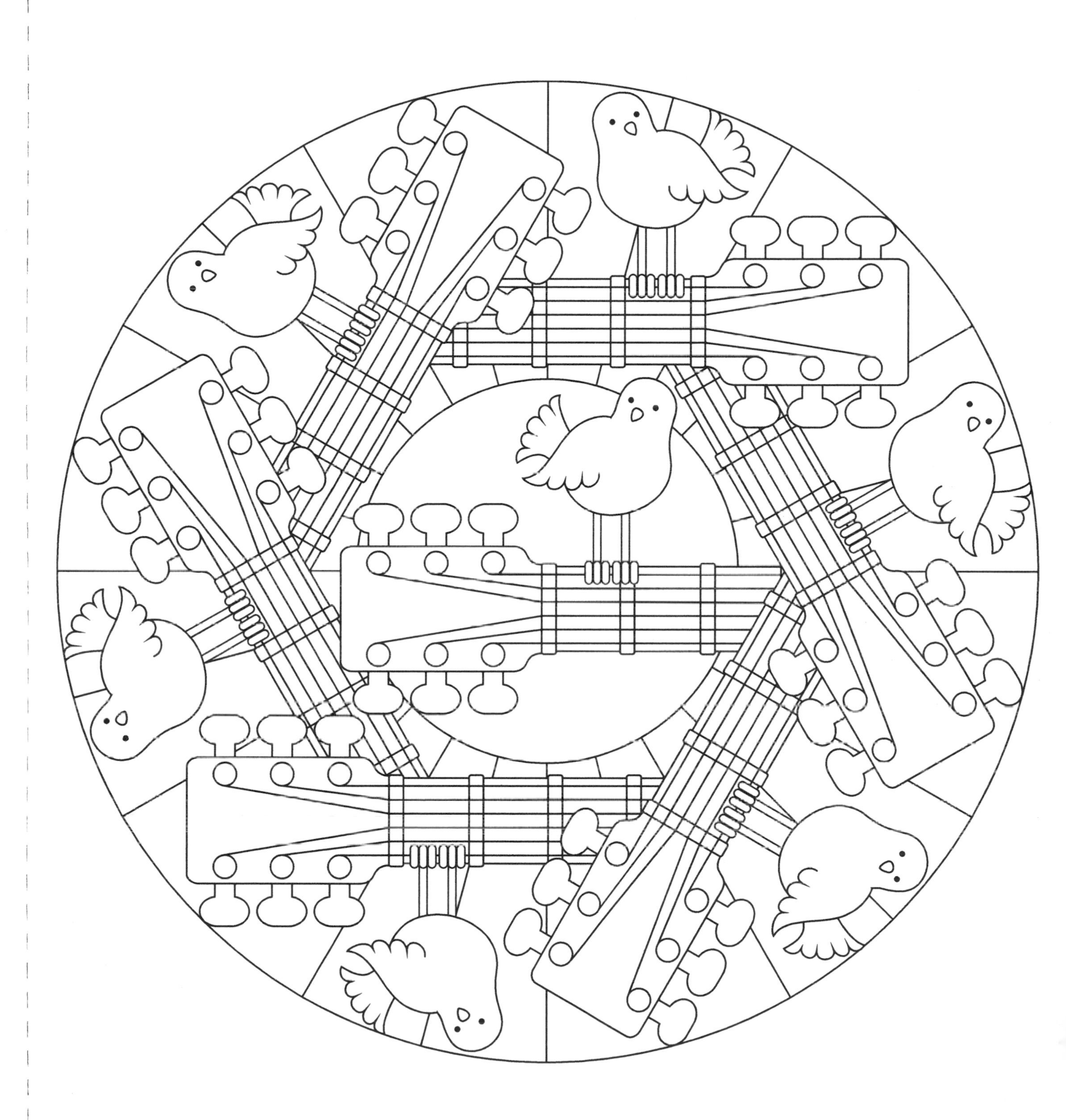

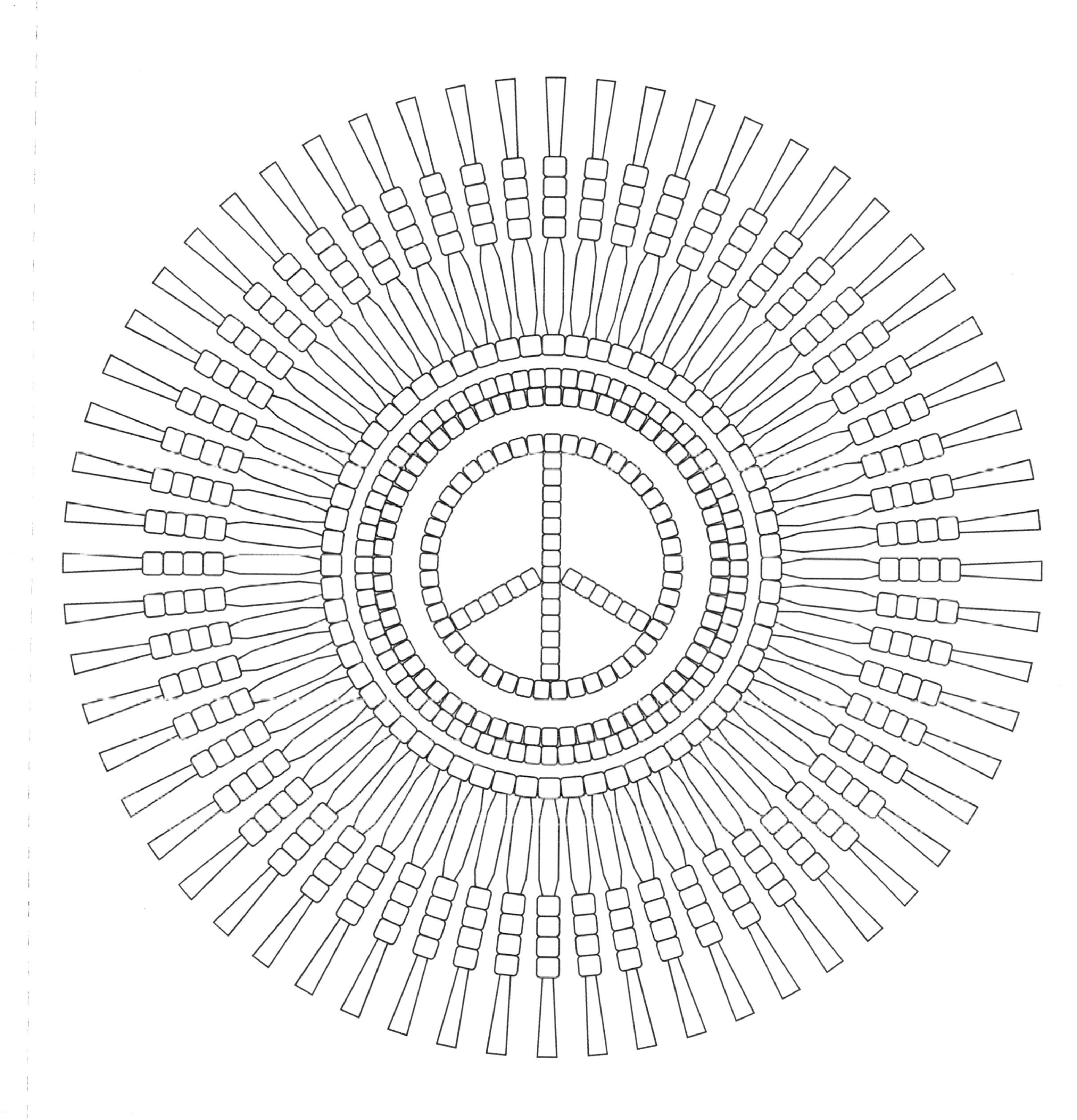

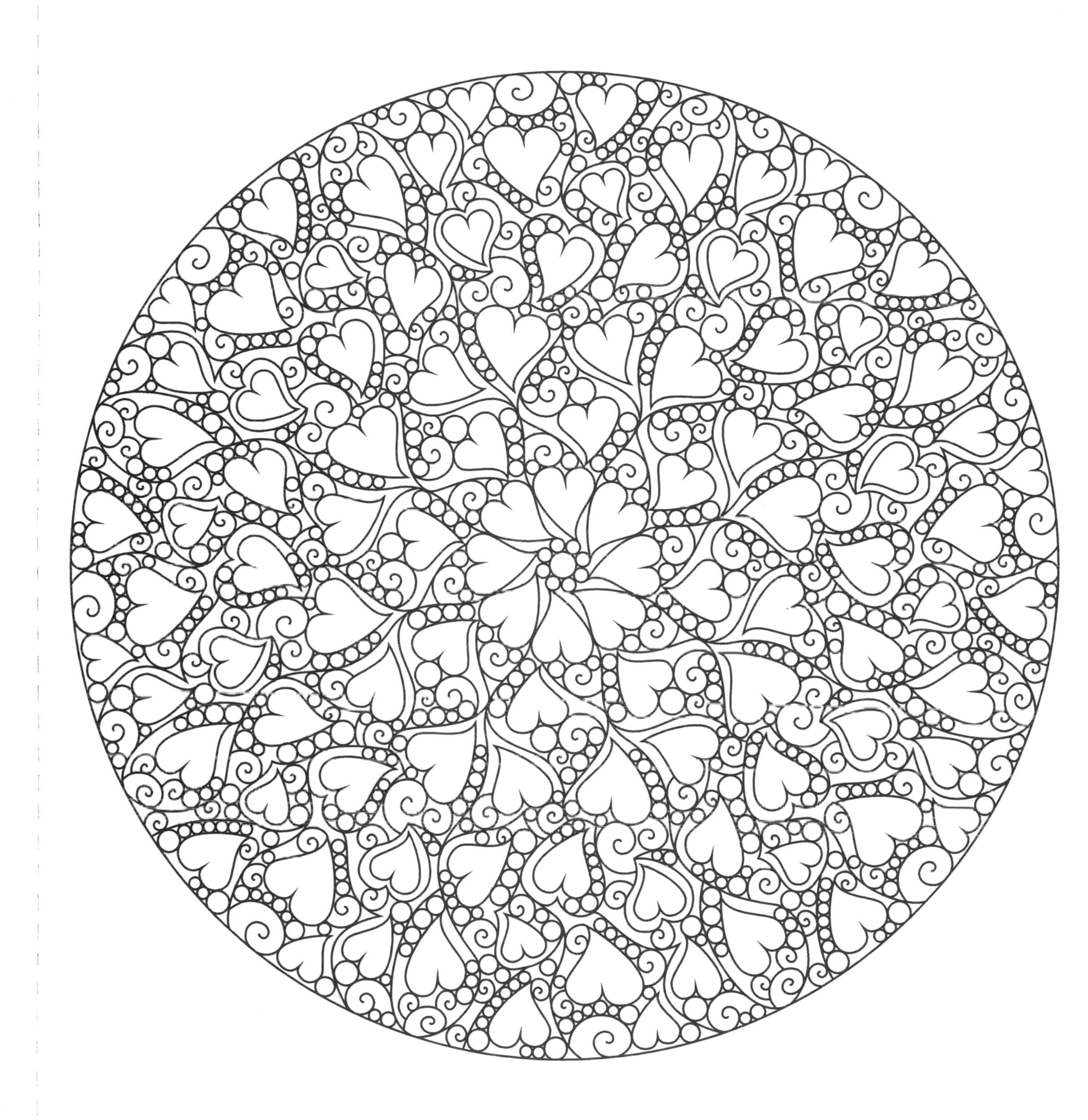

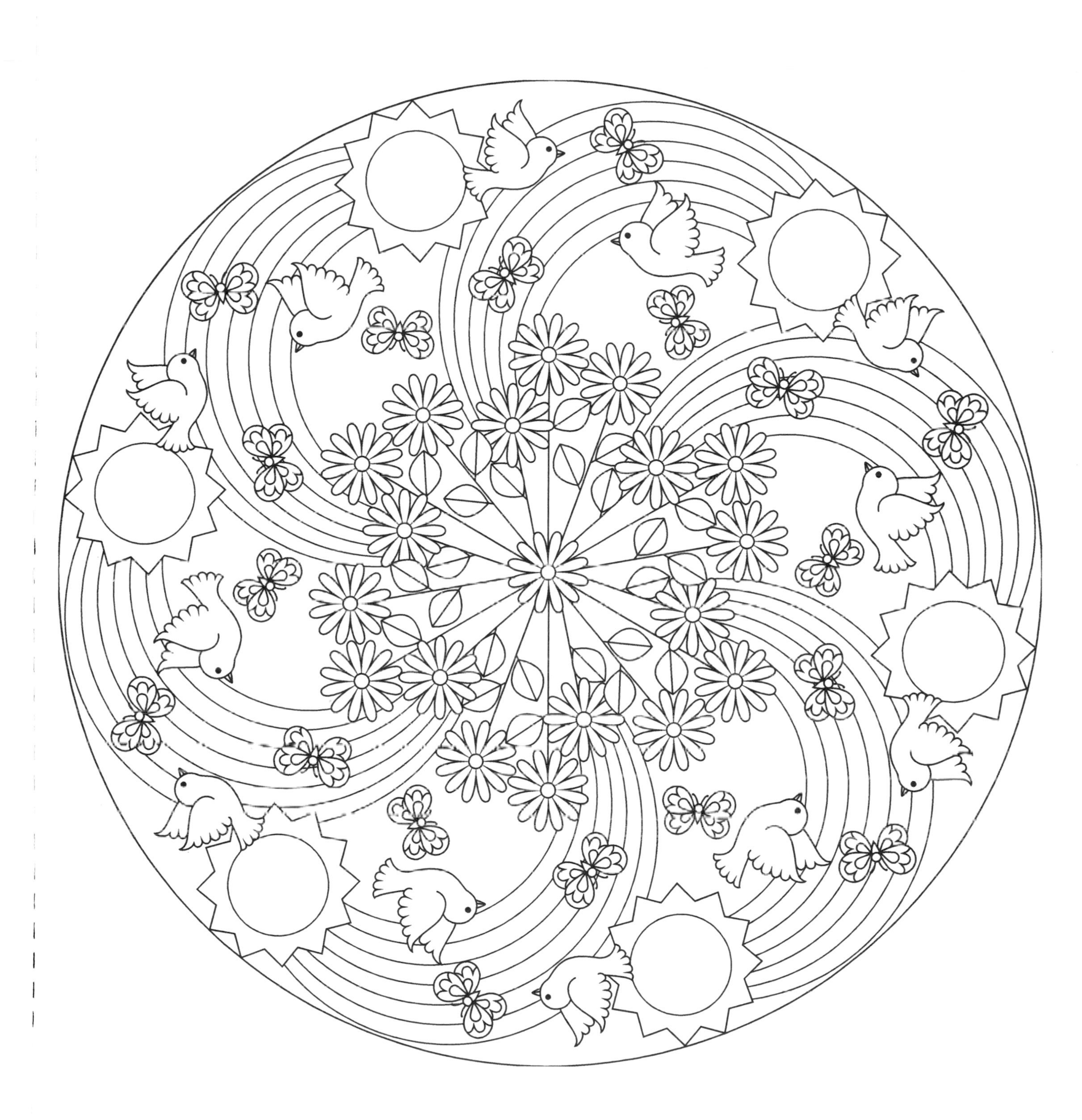